Bulldozers

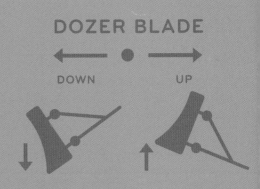
DOZER BLADE
DOWN   UP

Published by Creative Education
P.O. Box 227, Mankato, Minnesota 56002
Creative Education is an imprint of The Creative Company
www.thecreativecompany.us

Design and production by Rob & Damia Design
Art direction by Rita Marshall
Printed in the United States of America

Photographs by Alamy (Daily Grind, David Hoffman Photo Library,
Shire Pictures), Getty Images (Fox Photos, Lorentz Gullachsen, Alti Mar),
iStockphoto (Erin Castillo, Clayton Cole, Trevor Fisher, Chris Hellyar,
Julio de la Higuera, Brandon Laufenberg, Jason Lugo, Roger Milley,
Stan Rohrer, Lisa F. Young)

DIESEL
FUEL

Library of Congress Cataloging-in-Publication Data

Gilbert, Sara.
Bulldozers / by Sara Gilbert.
p. cm. — (Machines that build)
Includes index.
ISBN 978-1-58341-725-6
1. Bulldozers—Juvenile literature. I. Title. II. Series.

TA735.G55 2009
629.225—dc22   2007051660

First edition
9 8 7 6 5 4 3 2 1

ENGINE OIL

SEATBELTS

Bulldozers

sara gilbert
machines that build

A bulldozer is a big machine. It has a tall, wide blade in front. Sometimes it has a tool called a ripper in back. It moves on wide belts called crawler tracks. It is used to do many things.

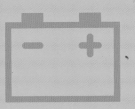

A bulldozer's blade is heavy and made of metal.

*Bulldozers can push dirt
and roll on top of it.*

Bulldozers move things. They push piles of dirt. They knock down trees. They move *rubble* out of the way. They get construction (*con-STRUK-shun*) sites ready for other machines to do their jobs.

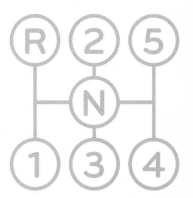

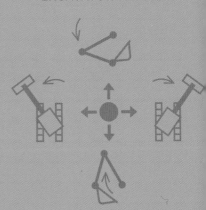

A bulldozer's blade can be

flat or curved.

It can even be changed to a
bucket to carry things.

The ripper looks like a giant claw.
It breaks up dirt and concrete.

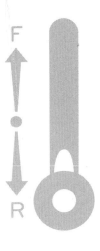

A bulldozer operator

An **operator** drives the bulldozer. The operator sits in the **cab**. He or she controls each crawler track separately. To turn, the operator uses a lever to make one track go forward. Another lever makes the other track go backward.

Some cabs have open sides without windows.

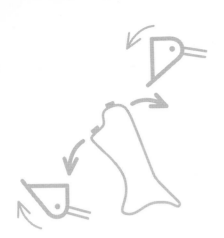

Farmers in America used the first bulldozers to clear their fields in the 1800s. The bulldozer blades were moved by donkeys instead of machines. In the early 1900s, the blades were put on tractors. By the 1930s, bulldozers had become strong machines.

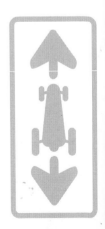

Bulldozers of long ago looked very different.

Bulldozers can be used almost anywhere.

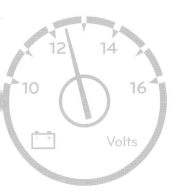

There are many different kinds of bulldozers. Some are big. Others are very small. Some can be used underwater or in swamps. Others work in mines and on ships.

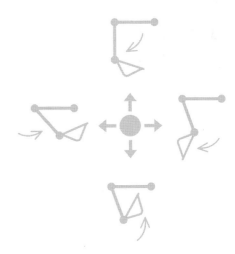

Underwater bulldozers are moved by *remote control*. Swamp bulldozers have long, wide crawler tracks. Mini dozers are small bulldozers. They have little blades. They can work in smaller places like gardens or parks.

People can use smaller bulldozers in parks.

Bulldozers can drive easily through mud and over rocks. They smooth out bumpy ground. They clear away trees and rubble. They make way for roads and buildings to be built!

A bulldozer can clear big rocks off of roads.

Activity: Be a Bulldozer

Make your hands into a bulldozer's blade, and push sand or dirt in your yard or at a park from one area to another. Now find some other "blades" like a paper plate, a small metal tray, and a piece of wood. Try pushing other objects, like blocks or books. What works the best? Which blade is the strongest?

Glossary

cab: the place where the operator sits

operator: the person who controls a machine

remote control: control of a machine from far away

rubble: broken pieces of stone, brick, and other things used to make buildings

steel: a strong material that is hard to break

Read More About It

Llewellyn, Claire. *Mighty Machines: Truck.* New York: DK Publishing, 2000.

Martin, M. T. *Bulldozers.* Minneapolis: Bellwether Media, 2007.

Index